John Monroe Johnson

Toss Repeat

SV

SurVision Books

First published in 2025 by
SurVision Books
Dublin, Ireland
Reggio di Calabria, Italy
www.survisionmagazine.com

Copyright © John Monroe Johnson, 2025

Cover image: "Xing Guard" by Brooke Holve

Design © SurVision Books, 2025

ISBN: 978-1-912963-57-7

This book is in copyright. No part of this publication may be reproduced, stored in a retrieval system, or transmitted in any form or by any means without the prior permission in writing from the publisher.

Acknowledgments

Grateful acknowledgment is made to the editors of the following, in which some of these poems, or versions of them, originally appeared:

Clade Song: "Science of Transposition and Cancellation"
frankmatter: "A Walk to the Beach"
Hidden Peak Press Spotlight: "Sooth Saying"
The Prose Poem: "To a Fault," "The Flop," "Variation," and "Criterion of Truth"
Right Hand Pointing: "Illusory Continuity of Tones" and "Persistence of Vision"
Sublunary Review: "As I Was Saying"
SurVision Magazine: "In a Time of Thirst"
Web Conjunctions: "Likely Story" and "Rithmetic"

In "In a Time of Thirst," *may your mustache grow like brushwood* is a Mongolian expression meaning *bless you. No hair on the tongue* is a Spanish expression meaning *straightforward. My eye went with me* is a Maltese expression meaning *I fell asleep.*

In "To a Fault," *to throw water at the ocean* is a Spanish expression meaning *to do something pointless. Fingernail and flesh* is the Spanish expression *uña y carne,* meaning figuratively *thick as thieves.*

In "Blur at the End," *nine cows and one strand of cow hair* is a Chinese expression meaning *a drop in the bucket.*

CONTENTS

Illusory Continuity of Tones	5
Text Hallucinations	6
Napping in Sample Space	7
Likely Story	8
The Flop	9
A Walk to the Beach	10
Criterion of Truth	11
In a Time of Thirst	12
A Radio Actor Prepares	13
Sympathetic Listener	14
Rithmetic	15
Dim the Lights	16
Sooth Saying	17
Your Polished Gladness	18
To a Fault	19
Call Center	20
Science of Transposition and Cancellation	21
Variation	22
Persistence of Vision	23
Vespers	24
Integer	25
Perturbation Theory	26
Toss Repeat	27
As I Was Saying	28
Blur at the End	29

Illusory Continuity of Tones

About to embark on a journey, a woman forgets her face in a mirror. She's in a hurry, ready to leave, but the simplest things keep falling into her hands. She looks up through a hole in the sky at a plane inventing itself in the mouth of a cloud. Soon the sun will climb down, infusing the air with allusion. Arrangements will be made, a list drawn up of things that go nameless. She'll commit to memory where she parked the car, but the machinery of cells, though they transcribe letter by letter, will disorder the copies so as to make them sticky and true.

Text Hallucinations

One day books in the library lose their punctuation. The librarian asks everyone to remain calm. Minutes later the punctuation returns. But for weeks the patrons go about the stacks on cloud feet.

Napping in Sample Space

Something happened just then, peculiar in the sense of riches in cattle. Trumpets, violins, oboes emitted sounds above our hearing. They made us heartsick but we couldn't prove it. Careful not to put our feet where the paint wasn't dry, we descended. Darkling beetles burrowed in the soil. A spear of grass tasted of asparagus. The minutes passed and a tide overtook our mattress. Now there was nowhere in sight, no place left to look out from. We were free but fretful, fretful as night herons roosting in daylight.

Likely Story

These are the days everyone talks about: pixilated skies, newness reinventing itself like an aura, each of us driving away. In Coeur d'Alene (Heart of an Awl) you fall in love with your eyes, enter the realm of the dead singing. But out here salmon and steelhead feint in heavy water. Monkey flowers, bleeding heart flowers, moments that clutch. Flies, too, attracted by the rotting meat fragrance certain flowers give off, saccades of day and night riddled with speech or thoughts of speech.

Beyond the pleural trees where the landscape breaks down, tidewater goby's drab little male makes a nursery of his mouth, contact calls the young. Daylight moon we can't see either sinks through salt brush, glasswort, with no idea. Meanwhile we're here, end of the loop, pausing by the gift shop on our way out of the grove, into exploding sunlight, relations who've never met. Equal and opposite, we seem to hold one another without touching, beat the drumhead air, try to get a word in. It was a pleasure. No, really. We've got to come back one day.

The Flop

She says, oh, let's not go over this again. Let me show you instead a woman at her desk with her fingers. See how the ceiling above her head opens and down come people on spider threads. This is her story, its telling phrases. According to one theory, she goes out to see a double feature at a former movie palace, in the former heart of a city. College friends squeeze into a tool shed in the dark which is cozy and fun until one of them leans against something sharp. There's a second balcony (closed). Shadows that must be bats dart across the screen. As she's leaving, she hears a rooster crow, but can't say where. It is her opinion she doesn't have one. You can bet her mother never left *her* in a shopping cart. "Once a gambler, always a gambler." She asks her mother, are you a gambler? "I used to be. They serve weak coffee here, but it's free. If you complain, you're supposed to put a dollar in the slot. We finish every session with a song. (That figures!): A bird in every hand. A period in every pot. The one inside never changes, only you do."

A Walk to the Beach

Where it lay, stranded, one pearl after another. Though it had all the strength it used to, it looked under the weather and didn't see us coming. Something was missing. It felt lonely with both hands. We were ready to help, but wanted fresh portions, wanted to serve, to make of it something special to gaze at with the horizon. We opened our eyes in time, but only just. That was fair. Over in one corner there were lights and lots of sounds. We turned toward them and it cost us. To liven is to unveil over and over, different each time, less some weight, say, or more patient as in following a vein with your fingers without knowing. I've always been bad with numbers, and a little thrilled. Now another hospital has closed, and I worry when I stand next to water without a meter stick or metronome. We're so caught up in the crisis in value, trochee and iamb, trunk and limb, we overlook the odd orange object, gust of wind that takes your hat.

Criterion of Truth

Alone in the reference room, we take another look at the record. Who doesn't like a good mystery. Bills of credit, bills of lading. Erasures that leave a mark. A suspect sets himself up, then dashes off. Disconnects the dots. He takes a touch of rain with him. Yellow iris. Almanac.

Blame it on speech balloons skewed to the extreme, although if I'm reading this right the planet sheds its past under pressure, for example near the mouths of thermal vents where giant tube worms and eyeless shrimp bear witness, which is another way of saying.

In a Time of Thirst

The horns of a cow led me to Mexico, to a place near trees where I spent the day in a ramshackle house half-hidden under apple-green leaves. My host (whose name escapes me) kept a small dog and a canary. Her English was eccentric and eerie. "I'm afraid I blunder the kiss." She had a mania for tracing birds and beasts. Their outlines were scattered everywhere. She said she liked sound ideas felt in the smallest places.

At lunch, she served a goose egg and poured two glasses. "May your mustache grow like brushwood!" (She had no hair on *her* tongue.) "I'll have another," I said, "in a French egg cup, if you please." There's truth in wine, every word's a sticking point. But I was losing body parts, and then *my eye went with me.* When I awoke, the devil was biting my head. I wondered, had I wandered at my peril again, thinking without learning.

A Radio Actor Prepares

Something stops your train of wheels. Could it be the cuckoo pecking at your rack and snail? The horologist takes your pulse. She can tell by the plewds that fly from your forehead that you apply yourself with vigor. Still, she checks for hobo signs. This could be the house of a dishonest man. "Have you been to Pittsburgh?" she asks (where so many careers come to an end, only to begin again). "No," you say. Nor do you mention the day, deep in rehearsal, when it all became clear, and you asked never to see yourself again, never to hear that discourse of internal noise whose author is never wholly known.

"What you get for chasing two rabbits," she says. Which may be why, during this cunicular year, you play in the escapement, witness marks on the flywheel attesting to ghosts and other pentimenti that gum the works. "Once upon a time Earth itself was unthinkable," she says, and writes you out a prescription. While at the dispensary (where the tip of the brush is everything) you encounter latrinalia. "The challenge lies in getting your eye into the eye of the movement." After a beat (timing, too, is everything) the "On Air" sign lights up over your head. Not since hair was romance have you felt such gusto.

Sympathetic Listener

Another night of sketchy props, skittish backdrops. A scout returns in silence, shaken by what he's seen. Getting old isn't as fun as it used to be. Not that it was ever a matter of time only. We go about our business, subjects in a thought experiment, hastened by the feeling-idea that, regardless of what has come before, this rent in the curtain is ours alone to pass through.

We gather in the kitchen where the conversation turns to the big game. "During commercials, I get up and walk around, try to avoid the influencers, but it's like swatting moonbats." A sympathy of clocks brings us to the edge of tears. Everyone expects one last drink, a kiss from the host, and some kind of perlage, a goody-bag that sorrow might enter as to a foundry and be transformed.

Rithmetic

Despite expectation, we reach morning like a milk bottle, elbows skinning, sweat beading. The poet warned us, "Do not think of numbers. They are a form of punishment." She held a book in her right hand, and with her left seemed to take something small from a dish and release it repeatedly. Thus we trembled in perseverating light, figured the attractive forces, took them in selectively, organs extending—never mind good intentions—everything truly remarkable without ever meaning to be so.

We met again outside the auditorium. Wasp-like our legs dangled because that's what keeps us blooming the shocked waters, dreaming up the right reader, whose incomplete transcript recommends them. It was Thursday. No perfections, no purposes. We thought we'd gotten ourselves out of the way. Ruby hyacinth in the city of love. Countless gradations of red.

Dim the Lights

Above the kitchen table floats a presence there's no explaining. Nothing of the original remains. If you press your ear to the base of a tumbler you might hear it passing. I wouldn't call it soul or spirit. A charge across two poles, perhaps. Arc of dependence. Or science.

Hush. The séance is about to begin.

Sooth Saying

You appear in a class photo of everyone you've ever known, garbled
    knot of your expression.
Your guide is a chance operation. Your colors, red and gold.
Your parents were pole-sitters, rag-pickers. They found you in a basket
    of gestures.
You've been keeping a scrapbook of sticks and grubs, swatches from a
    sanitary landfill.
Like certain numbers you are irrational, both guest and host, homesick
    for the road.
(No, that's not the sound of your heart. It's a misplaced modifier
    dangling.)
Afflicted by silence in rough concert, you walk past firefish without
    comment, poppies that tell the time of day.
Starbursts and visual snow are your warning signs.
You are *this close.*

Your Polished Gladness

You become impatient with the sky, its famous blue, the grief and nonsense it glosses, when a stretch of little noise fastens over you, and your mind, like a sea sponge passed through a sieve, wanders at once in all directions, ecstatic and incoherent, only to reassemble in the next instant, exactly as before.

There are those who swear they survived by going limp, who describe a pamphlet of love pressed hand to hand. But the heretic, what did the heretic choose? Mason bees in the rosemary. Segmented worms sifting with their flowery heads. Nothing sacred. Nothing despaired of.

To a Fault

Sorry I missed you. I was only just here, throwing water at the ocean. It's how I keep the doors open. "Buy like an angel," the sign says. But I worry about the business, its many tandems. Who was it said everything's already been said? We misjudge and the little psychosis ceases. You and I, though, we're fingernail and flesh, making space in our suitcase. You can count on it: the heart's ejection fraction knows something about travel, where ends meet. What I mean is, volume is not the same as gain. Here we are, another drought year, creek beds broken, the deer eating coffeeberry. Even the manzanita is having second thoughts. Toward the end of summer we'll have to shout above jets, then look where they've been, not where they are. Fortunately, we take the ocean with us. And childhood is inexhaustible. Anyway, we should try to arrange things if we can. I didn't mean to keep you waiting.

Call Center

It's May outside. Locust petals are falling like snow. The old scheduler's been let go. The new one ties a string around her finger. When do we start? When do we break for lunch? A few calls come in. They hang up before we answer. And when they don't, they don't say much. A grunt. A growl. Now it's raining. Of course that's good for trees. It reassures them. They want so much to be read to, to drink in the breath of our being. Lately though, I've been listening. Mostly it's what you'd expect: patter of bugs, hum of increase and decay. The weather won't settle. The sun moves from behind a cloud. A limb from one locust, caught in the fork of another, makes a noise like a humpback whale. Down the street a dog explains how it feels to spend the day behind a fence. The hours pass imperfectly. Habitual. Unfinished.

Science of Transposition and Cancellation

We've come to expect hard times in this city, where the wolf sings among the cantaloupes and ghost-like faces appear in the aisles, mouse of a muscle moving up and down, bending our efforts, kneeling wages. To ostracize a villain we write his name on potsherds of broken piggy banks. Something in the air grates against a market.

Speaking of other things, the divers brought home biscuits, twice-cooked, and abalone we meant to eat in peace, but the debt of being, so easily mistaken for appetite, went back and back, and the meal was called off. Even so, the naked mole rat lives underground forty years, free of cancer. And there's no accounting for human calculators, prime number savants.

Variation

Another day undone, and now evening is unbecoming. It had all been doable, taken in pieces, the processes interchangeable yet never indistinguishable, fluted chambers through which the impulse passed without diminishment, though its structure varied (bonds broken, electrons stripped from the outer shells), always something to read, something to watch while calibrating the image. Once you'd seen it your mind made up details. It's surprising how little it takes to suggest a figure, however difficult it may be to say what it is: human, fish, flower, above ground or below, fixed or free. For instance, here's a painting of an artist working *en plein air,* titled, "What the Eye Actually Sees." But the canvas in the painting is turned away, and the painter, behind it, peers back at the viewer. Or this one, a young caddy distracted by a luminous veil. Should he follow the old golfer onto the golden green? And this one, of only a few lines. The artist says, "The work comes from a sensation of pleasure." Maybe so. Then again, this may be more foolish fire. We'll have to watch with long eyes and see.

Persistence of Vision

It was about that time. We followed it down a deer path to a horseshoe bay where the wings of vinegar flies diffracted light in florescent colors. Everyone brought parasols and pink erasers. "That's nice," someone said. By which he meant ignorant or wanton, fastidious or shy or pleasant. Or something else.

They say the anemone opens under the influence of wind, and nearly everything, even concrete, is self-healing. That notwithstanding, there's an ullage needs looking into, a volume above. It follows first principles (primary shapes, Platonic solids). Like a flea comb it has fine teeth. Like an isometric exercise it pushes against itself and doesn't move.

Vespers

The architects are always home. Their falling bodies accelerate toward the bed of an ancient sea. Meanwhile, boomers fold back a tent flap, gaze out at Venus. They pray for a home-cooked meal prepared on another planet. "Poetry is translation," they say. Or is it, "Translation is poetry?" During the course of actual and imagined events stars reach out across the hoopla. A caterpillar climbs a twig and waits for judgement.

It happens behind your eyes, so you don't see, words on one side setting their hearts on the other. I eat and sleep, play quietly in the morning before anyone else is awake, look for what the cat left on the doormat. Has the day been short-listed? And what, if anything, will grow out of it, as music grows out of melody, tempo, the tension between repetition and randomness that touches us but keeps its distance?

Integer

In another ordinary loss of composure the heart flutters. Thought keeps lifting its head, saying, *I'm going out there. Maybe today we can cross the bridge of donkeys.* Common knowledge is helpful, but only to a point. Just a few wars ago they told my neighbor's son to enlist or go to jail. The court does not concern itself with minimal things. He got out of that one the hard way, while I went on living, a Swede on the sea. Around here, convention grows on trees.

But back to numbers. We let grass grow under them, then throw a zero in the bag. Nine to eleven, they add up. Sometimes, though, when the road starts slanting, they turn transcendental and you lose sight of them in the day-glow. I can't tell you how many times they've left me in the altogether, staring up at the Eye of Providence, pressing my thumbs. This much is certain: violins cut from old-growth trees sound different. Hardly a soul can hear them without weeping.

Perturbation Theory

The sun was setting eccentrically. We followed its arc erratically. At the sight of daisies everyone sighed, a sound like the cry of dust mites. Our house was one of many emergent properties. No one knew exactly how to address it. Two men in overalls walked through the foot of our bed. We waved our arms and shouted, but they acted as if we weren't there. Researchers said we were the exception that proved the rule, that we possessed a special ignorance that ought to be preserved and studied. In perilous times the intellect can be hard to pin down. It works itself to a pitch, then like a lazy eye looks away, saves for last the essential thing everyone knows it can't say.

Toss Repeat

The chance of a lifetime had us on edge. We thought we had it, and maybe we did, but it kept coming back in all its purposes. As if to catch us unawares it cupped its hands, and we heard the music no instrument makes. As with the speech-to-song illusion, we couldn't explain it.

Heavy rains in the Pacific Northwest. Gardens in the air. A salmon decomposing in a stream wakes inside the body of a redwood. In China they say, "Did a ghost make these marks? Is this a bird language?" You ask, "Is this a whale fall? Is it some signature event in the emergency of its unmaking?"

As I Was Saying

The water hammer kept us up last night. It seemed to know everyone there. As I approached the exit a woman asked if I had found everything I was looking for. Any second now it would all come back to her: how we'd met, what we'd meant to each other. Angels on the beach, with seaweed hair and sand dollar eyes, were turning shorebirds to stone. In the boardwalk arcade plastic moles popped up. A child beat them down delightedly. She was so small her father carried her in his coat pocket.

Blur at the End

Much in question this morning is last night's milky sea. So rare, as when a fossil floats to the surface, far from its origin yet perfectly preserved. How lucky we were to have sailed right through, contracting and expanding like jellies, with only a show of hands to guide us.

But what of the valued anchor, lost? The isopod that grips its host by the tongue? Textbooks offer an example: after a few years you can't even give them away. Regardless, we keep working toward you, *nine cows and one strand of cow hair.* Skin-deep. Dully glowing.

Selected Poetry Titles Published by SurVision Books

Contemporary Tangential Surrealist Poetry: An Anthology
Edited by Tony Kitt
ISBN 978-1-912963-44-7

Invasion: An Anthology of Ukrainian Poetry about the War
Edited by Tony Kitt
ISBN 978-1-912963-32-4

Noelle Kocot. *Humanity*
(New Poetics: USA)
ISBN 978-1-9995903-0-7

Marc Vincenz. *Einstein Fledermaus*
(New Poetics: USA)
ISBN 978-1-912963-20-1

Helen Ivory. *Maps of the Abandoned City*
(New Poetics: England)
ISBN 978-1-912963-04-1

Tony Kitt. *The Magic Phlute*
(New Poetics: Ireland)
ISBN 978-1-912963-08-9

Clayre Benzadón. *Liminal Zenith*
(New Poetics: USA)
ISBN 978-1-912963-11-9

Thomas Townsley. *Tangent of Ardency*
(New Poetics: USA)
ISBN 978-1-912963-15-7

Mikko Harvey & Jake Bauer. *Idaho Falls*
(Winner of James Tate Poetry Prize 2018)
ISBN 978-1-912963-02-7

Anton Yakovlev. *Chronos Dines Alone*
(Winner of James Tate Poetry Prize 2018)
ISBN 978-1-912963-01-0

John Bradley. *Spontaneous Mummification*
(Winner of James Tate Poetry Prize 2019)
ISBN 978-1-912963-13-3

Charles Kell. *Pierre Mask*
(Winner of James Tate Poetry Prize 2019)
ISBN 978-1-912963-19-5

John Thomas Allen. *Rolling in the Third Eye*
(Winner of James Tate Poetry Prize 2019)
ISBN 978-1-912963-15-7

Gary Glauber. *The Covalence of Equanimity*
(Winner of James Tate Poetry Prize 2019)
ISBN 978-1-912963-12-6

Tony Bailie. *Mountain Under Heaven*
(Winner of James Tate Poetry Prize 2019)
ISBN 978-1-912963-09-6

Alison Dunhill. *As Pure as Coal Dust*
(Winner of James Tate Poetry Prize 2020)
ISBN 978-1-912963-23-2

Charles Borkhuis. *Spontaneous Combustion*
(Winner of James Tate Poetry Prize 2021)
ISBN 978-1-912963-30-0

Noah Falck and Matt McBride. *Prerecorded Weather*
(Winner of James Tate Poetry Prize 2022)
ISBN 978-1-912963-39-3

Michael Zeferino Spring. *Kahlo's Window*
(Winner of James Tate Poetry Prize 2022)
ISBN 978-1-912963-40-9

Jeffrey Cyphers Wright. *Fuel for Love*
(Winner of James Tate Poetry Prize 2023)
ISBN 978-1-912963-45-4

George Kalamaras. *That Moment of Wept*
ISBN 978-1-9995903-7-6

George Kalamaras. *Through the Silk-Heavy Rains*
ISBN 978-1-912963-28-7

Ciaran O'Driscoll. *Angel Hour*
ISBN 978-1-912963-27-0

Guillaume Apollinaire. *Ocean of Earth: Selected Poems*
Translated from French by Matthew Geden
ISBN 978-1-912963-40-9

Maria Grazia Calandrone. *Fossils*
Translated from Italian
(New Poetics: Italy)
ISBN 978-1-9995903-6-9

Anton G. Leitner. *Selected Poems 1981–2015*
Translated from German
ISBN 978-1-9995903-8-3

Order our books from survisionmagazine.com

www.ingramcontent.com/pod-product-compliance
Lightning Source LLC
Chambersburg PA
CBHW061315040426
42444CB00010B/2656